PIES

↳ LAKELAND

Lakeland and ACP Magazines Ltd hereby exclude all liability to the extent permitted by law for any errors or omission in this book and for any loss, damage or expense (whether direct or indirect) suffered by a third party relying on any information contained in this book.

This book was created in 2010 for Lakeland by AWW Books, an imprint of Octopus Publishing Group Ltd, based on materials licensed to it by ACP Magazines Ltd, a division of PBL Media Pty Limited.

54 Park St, Sydney
GPO Box 4088, Sydney, NSW 2001
phone (02) 9282 8618; fax (02) 9267 9438
acpbooks@acpmagazines.com.au;
www.acpbooks.com.au

OCTOPUS PUBLISHING GROUP
Design – Chris Bell
Food Director - Pamela Clark

Published for Lakeland in the United Kingdom by Octopus Publishing Group Limited

Endeavour House
189 Shaftesbury Avenue
London WC2H 8JY
United Kingdom
phone + 44 (0) 207 632 5400;
fax + 44 (0) 207 632 5405
aww@octopusbooks.co.uk;
www.octopusbooks.co.uk
www.australian-womens-weekly.com

Printed and bound in China

A catalogue record for this book is available from the British Library.

ISBN 978-1-907428-12-8

The Department of Health advises that eggs should not be consumed raw. This book contains some dishes made with raw or lightly cooked eggs. It is prudent for vulnerable people such as pregnant and nursing mothers, invalids, the elderly, babies and young children to avoid uncooked or lightly cooked dishes made with eggs. Once prepared, these dishes should be kept refrigerated and used promptly.

This book also includes dishes made with nuts and nut derivatives. It is advisable for those with known allergic reactions to nuts and nut derivatives and those who may be potentially vulnerable to these allergies, such as pregnant and nursing mothers, invalids, the elderly, babies and children to avoid dishes made with nuts and nut oils. It is also prudent to check the labels of pre-prepared ingredients for the possible inclusion of nut derivatives.

Some of the recipes in this book have appeared in other publications.

PIES

There's something so heart-warming about a home-made pie hot from the oven. It's the complete meal in a dish and this cookbook is filled with 50 sweet and savoury suggestions. From cosy family suppers to exciting new pie recipes and elegant dessert tarts, each one is sure to be a tasty centrepiece for your table.

One of an exciting new series of cookbooks from Lakeland, *Pies* is packed with delicious colour photos and expert hints, tips and techniques for beginners and experienced cooks alike.

With every recipe triple-tested® for perfect results, these excellent cookbooks are sure to be some of the best-loved on your kitchen bookshelf. To discover the rest of the range, together with our unrivalled selection of creative kitchenware, visit one of our friendly Lakeland stores or shop online at www.lakeland.co.uk.

CONTENTS

TIPS & TECHNIQUES

TYPES OF PASTRY

Shortcrust pastry is the classic pastry used for pies. Work the butter into the flour using the fingertips until it resembles breadcrumbs, then add the liquid, usually egg and water, until the mixture forms a dough.

Making shortcrust pastry in the food processor is the preferred option of many cooks, but be careful not to overprocess. Use short, quick pulses when mixing the butter into the flour and be extra sparing with the water as it's harder to judge when the pastry is ready.

For step-by-step instructions for making shortcrust pastry, see pages 10–11.

Sweet short-crust pastry, as the name implies, has sugar added. If you use icing sugar instead of caster sugar you'll end up with a crisper pastry and avoid the possibility of a granular effect that occurs when sugar isn't dissolved.

Pâte sablée is another sweetened pastry, though more like a biscuit dough, in that the butter and sugar are beaten together before the flour and liquid are added. The word sablée means sandy or grainy and this effect is sometimes enhanced by the addition of ground almonds.

Puff pastry is truly a labour of love as it requires working the butter into the dough by repeated folding and rolling and resting the dough in the refrigerator between rolls to firm the butter (to keep the layers separate) and relax the gluten in the flour. If this sounds too much like hard work, the good news is that ready-rolled sheets of puff pastry are available in most supermarkets.

Reduced-fat puff pastry is also available, though it tends not to brown as well as the higher-fat version.

When using several sheets of pastry in a recipe, work with one sheet at a time, keeping the others in the freezer so that they don't become too soft.

Filo pastry Your life is probably too short to make your own filo pastry, but thankfully, these fine sheets of pastry are available in the freezer section of most supermarkets.

It is important to keep filo covered while you are working with it, as the thin sheets tend to dry out quickly and crumble or break. To prevent this happening, cover the pastry completely with cling film or baking parchment, then a well wrung-out damp tea towel. If the pastry does break up, don't panic. It's actually quite forgiving and as you are usually working in layers, any minor tears will be covered and not be visible in the final product.

HANDLING PASTRY

Kneading This really means turning the outside edges of the dough into the centre. When applied to most pastries it's not the heavy action you might apply to breadmaking, just lightly working the dough into a manageable shape.

Rolling We find it's best to roll out pastry between sheets of baking parchment or greaseproof paper or cling film. If you work on a floured surface with a floured rolling pin, there's always the risk that you'll upset the balance of ingredients by working in too much flour. Besides, it's easier to pick up a sheet of pastry and transfer it to the pie dish when there's a sheet of paper or plastic supporting it.

Start rolling with short light strokes from the centre outwards, each time rolling the pastry towards you then away from you. Reduce the pressure towards the edges and don't roll over the edges.

Pastry is best rolled on a cold surface; marble is perfect, but your worktop will be fine, so long as it's smooth and clean.

Resting Always let pastry rest, wrapped in cling film or a plastic bag, in the refrigerator for up to 30 minutes before rolling and after lining the dish and covering the pie. This allows the gluten (protein) in the flour to relax and prevents the pastry from shrinking too much during baking.

STORING AND FREEZING

Pastry can be stored, wrapped securely in cling film or a plastic bag in the refrigerator for one or two days, or frozen for up to two months. When freezing, be sure to label with a use-by date. To defrost, place overnight in the refrigerator and return to room temperature before rolling. You can also freeze, lined, unbaked pastry cases. Thaw as above.

Frozen pies To reheat a frozen or refrigerated pie: defrost in the refrigerator, then bring to room temperature before baking. If the pie has already been baked and just needs reheating, place it in a slow oven until warmed through.

BAKING BLIND

Pastry cases which are to be filled with a cold filling are usually baked 'blind', that is empty. Cases in which the filling is cooked are often partially baked blind to ensure the pastry stays crisp when the filling is added. As a general rule of thumb to avoid a soggy base, add hot fillings to hot cases and cold fillings to cold, just before serving.

To bake blind, line the pastry case with a piece of baking parchment, or unwaxed greaseproof paper cut a few centimetres larger than the circumference of the flan. Fill the paper with dried beans, uncooked rice, lentils or purpose-made ceramic pastry weights to stop the pastry from rising during cooking. Place the flan pan on an oven tray and bake in a moderately hot oven for 10 minutes or as the recipe specifies. Remove the paper and beans carefully. (Store the cooled beans in a container marked for future baking as you won't be able to cook them after they have been in the oven.) Either add the filling at this stage, or continue baking as directed by the recipe. For step-by-step instructions to blind baking, see pages 12–13.

Some cooks swear by lining their flan cases with foil which they maintain conducts heat well and results in a crisper base. Others sprinkle the case with dry cake crumbs or fine soft breadcrumbs before adding a fruit mixture, to soak up any excess liquid.

LINING PIE AND FLAN DISHES

To line a pie dish Roll out the bottom layer of pastry to allow about a 2cm overhang on the dish. Drape the pastry over the rolling pin and transfer it to the dish, easing it in gently to avoid stretching it. If it does happen to break, don't panic – you can usually patch up a pastry tear with an offcut. Press the pastry evenly over the base of the pie dish, make sure that no air is trapped between the pastry and the dish by using your fingers or a small ball of pastry dipped in flour. Fill with prepared filling. Roll out the pastry lid to about 2cm larger than the pie dish, moisten the outer edge of the base pastry, then drape the lid over the filling. Press the edges together firmly without stretching the pastry. Holding the pie dish in one hand and a sharp knife in the other, trim off the overhanging pastry, angling the knife slightly under the rim as you turn the dish around.

Pie lids are often brushed with egg, or an egg and milk mixture to glaze and help brown the tops.

One-crust pies have a lid but no base. The filling is placed in a container just large enough to hold it. If the filling is not firm enough to mound, you can support the lid by placing a pie funnel or upsidedown egg cup in the centre of the pie. A pie funnel or a pastry bird will serve the added role of venting the pie – through the bird's 'mouth'. Alternatively, cut a few slashes in the pastry to allow the steam to escape.

To cover a one-crust pie, roll out the pastry to about 4cm larger than the top of the dish; cut a 1cm strip from the outside of the pastry and place the strip around the rim of the pie dish. Moisten the pastry rim, using the rolling pin, lay the pastry lid over the pie dish, pressing together the pastry strip and lid, without stretching the pastry. Trim any excess using the method described for two-crust pies.

To line a flan tin Drape the pastry over a lightly floured rolling pin and position it on the tin. Gently ease the pastry into the tin, pressing with your fingers or thumb to ensure that no air pockets develop. Roll the rolling pin across the top edge of the flan tin to trim the pastry evenly. Rest the pastry as specified in the recipe to prevent it from shrinking during cooking.

Where the recipe indicates, prick or 'dock' the base of the pastry with a fork. This will help prevent the pastry developing air bubbles during baking. Keep an eye on it while it's cooking and if it does rise, you can flatten the

bump by pressing gently with the back of a spoon or a ball of rolled up (clean) tea towel or a ball of floured scrap pastry.

TYPES OF PIE DISHES

Practically any ovenproof vessel with raised sides can be used as a pie dish. Traditional pie dishes are usually made of ceramic, thin enamelled metal or heat-resistant glass. Ceramic dishes are ideal for pies that have lots of filling as they take up the heat gradually and heat the filling slowly and evenly.

Free-form or rustic pies require no dish at all as they are simply baked on an oven tray. The filling is placed in the centre of the pastry with an overlap on all sides which is folded over to partially enclose the filling.

SHORTCRUST PASTRY STEP BY STEP

SIFTING

Sifting isn't essential, but it's what we pastry-makers do. Use a sifter or a strainer to sift the dry ingredients into a wide-topped bowl. Chill the bowl if making pastry on a hot day.

RUBBING-IN BUTTER

Chop chilled butter into cubes, use your fingertips (the coolest part of your hands) to squash butter cubes through the flour. Do this quickly to keep the butter cold. Shake the bowl so any large lumps come to the surface.

ADDING EGG YOLK

Egg yolks are not always added to shortcrust pastry, but they do add colour and richness from the added fat. Egg yolks are best if refrigerator-cold. Add it now, but don't mix it in yet.

KNEADING DOUGH

Turn the dough onto a cold surface, then barely knead the dough until the ingredients are gathered together, and almost smooth. Don't over-handle the dough, it will toughen the dough and make it difficult to handle.

RESTING DOUGH

It's important to rest the dough in the fridge for about 30 minutes. Pat dough into a flat shape, wrap in cling film, and place it in the fridge. Put the timer on as too long in the fridge will make the dough hard to roll out and you will have to let in stand for a while before rolling.

PROCESSOR PASTRY

Food processors make really good pastry, and are particularly useful if the pastry-maker has hot hands. Put the dry ingredients into the bowl of the processor, no need for sifting, add the chopped chilled butter.

ADDING LEMON JUICE

If you're adding egg yolk to the dough, most recipes will use lemon juice to counteract the richness of the egg yolk. Use freshly squeezed lemon juice, then strain it.

ADDING LIQUID

If you want a shortcrust pastry that is not so rich, use chilled water in place of the egg yolk and lemon juice. Follow whatever the recipe suggests. Most recipes will suggest an approximate amount of water.

COMBINING INGREDIENTS

Use the fingertips of one hand to gently, lightly and quickly pull the ingredients together. You should have just enough liquid to moisten the dry ingredients.

PROCESSING

Pulse the ingredients until the butter has barely cut through the flour. Don't walk away and leave the processor on, as the blade will continue to cut the butter through the flour, and the ingredients will come together. It's important to add some liquid to the dough.

PULSING

Add enough of the liquid to the flour/butter mixture. Only experience will teach you how much to add – the same as if you were making pastry by hand. Pulse the ingredients until the processor works them into a ball. Remove the dough from the processor.

RESTING PROCESSOR PASTRY

Knead the dough until it's smooth, as above. It's just as important to rest the processor-made pastry, as it is to rest the hand-made pastry. Processor pastry usually looks smoother than hand-made pastry because the butter has been cut through the flour more evenly.

BAKING BLIND STEP BY STEP

ROLLING
Roll the chilled rested pastry from the centre to the edge between sheets of baking parchment or greaseproof paper or cling film. This method is clean, neat and easy.

LINING
Peel away the top layer of paper, then turn the pastry into the tin etc. Gently peel away the remaining sheet of paper, allowing the pastry to fall into the tin. Ease the pastry into the shape of the tin without stretching it.

SHAPING
Use a small scrap of pastry, pressed into a ball, then lightly floured, to gently push the pastry around the inside of the pie tin – don't stretch the pastry.

WEIGHTING
Use enough dried beans (or any kind of pulse) or uncooked rice to fill the pastry case and weigh the pastry down. These ingredients cannot be used for any other purpose, other than blind baking. Keep the beans etc., in a glass jar until next time.

BAKING
Recipes will tell you how long the pastry case needs to bake. This is done in two stages: the first with the paper and beans, and the second without the paper and beans.

AIR BUBBLES
If the pastry develops an air bubble during the first 5 to 10 minutes of baking, press the bubble gently with a ball of scrap pastry. If you leave if too long to squash the bubble(s), the pastry will cook too much and break on squashing.

TRIMMING

If the tin has a sharp edge, like a fluted flan tin, simply roll the rolling pin over the top edge of the tin. The pressure from the rolling pin will cut the excess pastry away cleanly.

DOCKING

Some pastry cases, depending on the type of filling to be used, are docked to stop them rising when they're baked. Do this by pricking the pastry all over with a fork, or by rolling a pastry docker (as shown) over the pastry case.

LINING

Line the pastry case with a piece of baking parchment, greaseproof paper or foil strong enough to hold the weight of the beans or rice etc, and large enough to hold and remove from the tin.

COVERING

Some recipes will direct you to blind bake a pastry case, then fill it, then top it with another layer of pastry. This method is good for pies with a wet filling, such as fruit and meat pies – it decreases the chance of a soggy pastry case.

TRIMMING

Hold the pie plate, flat on one hand, at eye level, then, using a sharp knife, and a downward cutting action, trim away the excess pastry, at a 45° angle.

SEALING

Use a fork, spoon etc to decorate the edge of the pie. Glaze the pastry as directed in the recipe, then slash some holes in the top of the pastry to allow steam to escape.

SAVOURY PIES

SNAPPER & FENNEL PIES

4 medium spring onions (100g
40g butter
1 large fennel bulb (550g), sliced
  thinly
2 tablespoons plain flour
250ml fish stock
125ml single cream
2 tablespoons finely chopped
  fennel tops or dill
2 teaspoons dijon mustard
1 tablespoon lemon juice
30g frozen peas
4 x 200g snapper fillets, chopped
  coarsely (or any white fish fillet)
2 sheets butter puff pastry
1 egg, beaten lightly

1 Trim spring onions, leaving about 6cm of the stem. Slice thinly.
2 Melt butter in large frying pan; cook onion and fennel, stirring, until onion softens.
3 Add flour to frying pan; cook, stirring, 1 minute. Gradually stir in stock and cream; cook, stirring, until sauce boils and thickens. Stir in fennel tops, mustard, juice and peas. Add fish, stir to combine; remove from heat.
4 Preheat oven to 200°C/180°C fan-assisted.
5 Spoon mixture into four 375ml ovenproof dishes; place on oven tray.
6 Cut four 2cm-wide strips from pastry. Cut four pastry lids large enough to fit the tops of the dishes. Brush dish edges with egg, place pastry strips around edge of dishes; top with pastry lids. Brush with a little more egg.
7 Bake pies about 35 minutes or until pastry is puffed and browned.

prep + cook time 1 hour
makes 4
nutritional count per pie
46.9g fat; 788 cal (3294kJ)

CREAMY FISH PIE

10g butter
2 teaspoons olive oil
1 small brown onion (80g),
   chopped finely
1 medium carrot (120g), chopped
   finely
1 stalk celery (150g), trimmed,
   chopped finely
1 tablespoon plain flour
250ml fish stock
500g firm white fish fillets,
   chopped coarsely
125ml single cream
1 tablespoon english mustard
120g frozen peas
40g finely grated parmesan
   cheese
1 sheet puff pastry
1 egg, beaten lightly

1 Preheat oven to 220°C/200°C fan-assisted.
2 Melt butter with oil in large saucepan; cook onion, carrot and celery, stirring, until carrot softens. Stir in flour; cook, stirring, 2 minutes. Add stock and fish; cook, stirring, until fish is cooked through and mixture boils and thickens. Remove from heat; stir in cream, mustard, peas and cheese.
3 Spoon mixture into a shallow small 1.5-litre baking dish; top with pastry. Brush top with egg.
4 Bake pie about 20 minutes or until browned.

prep + cook time 40 minutes
serves 4
nutritional count per serving
35.1g fat; 566 cal (2366kJ)
tip It is important to use a shallow baking dish so that the top of the fish mixture is touching the pastry and the pastry is not stuck to the sides of the dish, as this could prevent it from rising

SHEPHERD'S PIE

30g butter
1 medium brown onion (150g),
   chopped finely
1 medium carrot (120g), chopped
   finely
½ teaspoon dried mixed herbs
750g chopped cooked lamb
70g tomato paste
60ml tomato sauce
2 tablespoons worcestershire
   sauce
500ml beef stock
2 tablespoons plain flour
80ml water
potato topping
5 medium potatoes (1kg),
   chopped
60g butter, chopped
60ml milk

1 Preheat oven to 200°C/180°C fan-assisted. Oil shallow 2.5-litre ovenproof dish.
2 Make potato topping.
3 Heat butter in large saucepan; cook onion and carrot, stirring, until tender. Add mixed herbs and lamb; cook, stirring, 2 minutes. Stir in paste, sauces and stock, then blended flour and water; stir over heat until mixture boils and thickens. Pour mixture into dish.
4 Place heaped tablespoons of potato topping on lamb mixture. Bake about 20 minutes or until browned lightly and heated through.
potato topping Boil, steam or microwave potatoes until tender; drain. Mash with butter and milk until smooth.

prep + cook time 1 hour
serves 4
nutritional count per serving
36.2g fat; 712 cal (2976kJ)

LIVER, BACON & MUSHROOM PIES

500g lamb's liver
2 tablespoons olive oil
1 clove garlic, crushed
1 medium brown onion (150g),
  chopped finely
4 rashers rindless bacon (260g),
  chopped coarsely
200g button mushrooms,
  quartered
2 tablespoons plain flour
125ml dry red wine
375ml beef stock
1kg packet frozen french fries
1 sheet puff pastry
1 egg yolk
1 tablespoon milk

1 Preheat oven to 220°C/200°C fan-assisted. Line oven tray with baking parchment.
2 Discard membrane and any fat from liver; chop coarsely. Heat half of the oil in large frying pan; cook liver, in batches, over high heat until browned and cooked as desired.
3 Heat remaining oil in same pan; cook garlic, onion, bacon and mushrooms, stirring, until onion softens. Add flour; cook, stirring, until mixture thickens and bubbles. Gradually add wine and stock; stir until mixture boils and thickens. Return liver to pan.
4 Meanwhile, cook fries, in oven, according to packet instructions.
5 Cut four 9.5cm rounds from pastry sheet; place on tray, brush with combined egg and milk. Bake, uncovered, with chips about 5 minutes or until rounds are browned lightly.
6 Divide liver mixture among four 310ml ramekins; top with pastry rounds, serve with fries.

prep + cook time 35 minutes
serves 4
nutritional count per serving
60.2g fat; 1326 cal (5543kJ)

EGG & BACON PIE

320g wholemeal plain flour
150g white plain flour
200g cold butter, chopped
1 egg
2 tablespoons iced water,
  approximately
2 teaspoons olive oil
1 large onion (200g), chopped
10 rashers rindless bacon (650g),
  chopped
8 eggs, extra
250g grated cheddar cheese
3 tablespoons chopped fresh
  chives
1 egg yolk

1 Grease deep 25cm round pie dish. Sift flours into bowl, rub in butter (or process flours and butter until mixture resembles breadcrumbs). Add egg and enough water to make ingredients cling together (or process until ingredients just come together). Press dough into a ball, knead on floured surface until smooth. Wrap in cling film; refrigerate 30 minutes.
2 Roll two-thirds of the pastry between sheets of baking parchment until large enough to line dish. Lift pastry carefully into dish; ease into side, trim edge. Prick base with fork; cover, refrigerate 30 minutes.
3 Preheat oven to 200°C/180°C fan-assisted.
4 Line pastry with baking parchment, fill with dried beans or rice; place on oven tray. Bake 10 minutes. Remove paper and beans; bake further 10 minutes or until browned. Cool.
5 Reduce oven to 180°C/160°C fan-assisted.
6 Heat oil in medium frying pan; cook onion and bacon, stirring, until onion is soft.

7 Break an extra egg into a cup, gently pour unbeaten egg into pastry case. Repeat with remaining eggs. Top with bacon mixture and combined cheese and chives.
8 Roll remaining pastry until large enough to cover pie. Brush edge of pie with egg yolk, carefully lift pastry onto pie; trim edge carefully.
9 Bake pie about 45 minutes or until browned.

prep + cook time 1 hour 30 minutes (+ refrigeration)
serves 6
nutritional count per serving
57.5g fat; 913 cal (3816kJ)

STEAK & KIDNEY PIE

300g beef kidneys
1.5kg beef braising steak,
  chopped coarsely
2 medium brown onions (300g),
  sliced thinly
250ml beef stock
1 tablespoon soy sauce
35g plain flour
125ml water
2 sheets puff pastry
1 egg, beaten lightly

1 Remove fat from kidneys; chop kidneys finely. Place kidneys, steak, onion, stock and sauce in large saucepan; simmer, covered, about 1 hour or until steak is tender.
2 Preheat oven to 200°C/180°C fan-assisted.
3 Stir blended flour and water into beef mixture; stir until mixture boils and thickens. Transfer to 1.5-litre ovenproof dish.
4 Cut pastry into 6cm rounds. Overlap rounds on beef mixture; brush with egg. Bake pies about 15 minutes or until browned.

prep + cook time 1 hour 50 minutes
serves 6
nutritional count per serving 25.8g fat; 609 cal (2546kJ)

CHUNKY BEEF & VEGETABLE PIE

1 tablespoon olive oil

1.5kg stewing beef, cut into 2cm pieces

60g butter

1 medium brown onion (150g), chopped finely

1 clove garlic, crushed

35g plain flour

250ml dry white wine

750ml hot beef stock

2 tablespoons tomato paste

2 stalks celery (200g), trimmed, cut into 2cm pieces

2 medium potatoes (400g), cut into 2cm pieces

1 large carrot (180g), cut into 2cm pieces

1 large courgette (150g), cut into 2cm pieces

150g mushrooms, quartered

120g frozen peas

6 tablespoons finely chopped fresh flat-leaf parsley

2 sheets puff pastry

1 egg, beaten lightly

1 Heat oil in large saucepan; cook beef, in batches, until browned all over. Remove from pan.

2 Melt butter in same pan; cook onion and garlic, stirring, until onion softens. Add flour; cook, stirring, until mixture thickens and bubbles. Gradually stir in wine and stock; stir until mixture boils and thickens slightly.

3 Return beef to pan with paste, celery, potato and carrot; bring to the boil. Reduce heat; simmer, covered, 1 hour.

4 Add courgette and mushrooms; simmer, uncovered, about 30 minutes or until beef is tender. Add peas; stir until heated through. Remove from heat; stir in parsley.

5 Preheat oven to 220°C/200°C fan-assisted.

6 Divide warm beef mixture between two deep 25cm pie dishes; brush outside edge of dishes with a little egg. Top each pie with a pastry sheet; pressing edges to seal. Trim pastry; brush pastry with egg.

7 Bake about 20 minutes or until browned.

prep + cook time 2 hours 20 minutes
serves 8
nutritional count per serving 27.6g fat; 577 cal (2412kJ)

BEEF TURNOVERS

1 tablespoon olive oil
2 medium brown onions (300g),
    chopped coarsely
800g minced beef
2 medium carrots (240g),
    chopped coarsely
35g plain flour
750ml beef stock
185g frozen peas
140g frozen corn kernels
6 sheets puff pastry
1 egg, beaten lightly

1 Heat oil in large heavy-based saucepan; cook onion, stirring, until soft. Add beef; cook, stirring, until beef changes colour. Add carrot, and blended flour and stock; cook, stirring, until mixture boils and thickens. Stir in peas and corn; cool.
2 Cut six 18cm rounds from pastry. Join pastry scraps; cut two more 18cm rounds.
3 Preheat oven to 220°C/200°C fan-assisted.
4 Divide filling equally among rounds; brush edge lightly with egg. Fold pastry over to enclose filling, press edges together to seal. Brush turnovers, both sides, with egg; place on lightly oiled oven trays.
5 Bake, uncovered, about 20 minutes or until pastry is browned and turnovers are heated through.Serve with homemade tomato sauce.

prep + cook time 50 minutes
serves 8
nutritional count per serving
21.1g fat; 390 cal (1635kJ)

BEEF CARBONADE PIES

2kg beef braising steak, diced
   into 3cm pieces
75g plain flour
40g butter, melted
60ml vegetable oil
4 medium brown onions (600g),
   sliced thickly
2 large carrots (360g), chopped
   coarsely
2 cloves garlic, crushed
680ml stout
2 tablespoons brown sugar
60ml cider vinegar
3 sprigs fresh thyme
1 bay leaf
3 sheets puff pastry
1 tablespoon milk
1 egg, beaten lightly

1 Coat beef in flour; shake off excess. Heat butter and 2 tablespoons of the oil in large deep saucepan; cook beef, in batches, until browned all over. Remove from pan.

2 Heat remaining oil in same pan; cook onion, carrot and garlic, stirring, until onion softens. Return beef to pan with stout, sugar, vinegar, thyme and bay leaf; bring to the boil. Reduce heat; simmer, covered, 1½ hours.

3 Uncover; simmer, stirring occasionally, about 1 hour or until beef is tender and sauce thickens. Discard herbs.

4 Preheat oven to 220°C/200°C fan-assisted.

5 Spoon beef mixture into six 430ml ovenproof dishes. Cut each pastry sheet into two pieces, large enough to top each dish. Brush pastry with combined milk and egg; place dishes on oven tray.

6 Bake pies about 15 minutes or until pastry is puffed and browned lightly.

prep + cook time 3 hours
serves 6
nutritional count per serving 33.9g fat; 701 cal (2930kJ)

CHICKEN & LEEK PIE

500ml chicken stock
600g chicken breast fillets
1 tablespoon olive oil
40g butter
1 large leek (500g), sliced thinly
2 stalks celery (300g), trimmed,
   chopped finely
2 tablespoons plain flour
2 teaspoons fresh thyme leaves
125ml milk
250ml single cream
2 teaspoons wholegrain mustard
2 sheets shortcrust pastry
1 sheet puff pastry
1 egg yolk

1 Bring stock to the boil in medium saucepan. Add chicken; return to the boil. Reduce heat; simmer, covered, about 10 minutes or until chicken is cooked. Remove from heat; stand chicken in poaching liquid 10 minutes. Remove chicken; chop coarsely. Reserve 80ml of the poaching liquid; keep remainder for another use, or discard.

2 Heat oil and butter in medium saucepan; cook leek and celery, stirring, until leek softens. Add flour and thyme; cook, stirring, 1 minute. Gradually stir in reserved poaching liquid, milk and cream; cook, stirring, until mixture boils and thickens. Stir in chicken and mustard. Cool 10 minutes.

3 Preheat oven to 200°C/180°C fan-assisted. Oil 1.5-litre ovenproof pie dish.

4 Line base and side of dish with shortcrust pastry, trim to fit; prick well all over with fork. Bake 10 minutes. Cool 5 minutes.

5 Spoon chicken mixture into pastry case; place puff pastry over filling, trim to fit dish. Brush pastry with egg yolk; cut two small slits in top of pastry. Bake about 20 minutes or until browned lightly.

prep + cook time 1 hour
35 minutes
serves 6
nutritional count per serving
56g fat; 800 cal (3344kJ)

SWEET PIES

QUINCE & RHUBARB PIE

500ml water
440g caster sugar
4 medium quinces (1.2kg),
  peeled, quartered
2 strips lemon rind
500g rhubarb, chopped coarsely
60ml lemon juice, approximately
150g plain flour
55g icing sugar
100g cold butter, chopped
1 egg, separated
1 tablespoon iced water,
  approximately
1 tablespoon golden granulated
  sugar

1 Stir the water and sugar in medium saucepan over low heat until sugar has dissolved. Add quince and rind; bring to the boil. Reduce heat; simmer, covered, about 2 hours, or until quinces are tender and a rosy colour. Add rhubarb; cook 5 minutes or until rhubarb softens. Add juice to taste, to reduce sweetness. Cool quince and rhubarb in the syrup.

2 Meanwhile, process flour, icing sugar and butter until crumbly. Add egg yolk and iced water, process until ingredients just come together. Knead gently on floured surface until smooth. Cover; refrigerate 30 minutes.

3 Preheat oven to 180°C/160°C fan-assisted. Grease 23cm pie dish.

4 Drain fruit mixture, reserving 80ml of the syrup. Spoon fruit mixture and reserved syrup into prepared dish.

5 Roll out pastry until large enough to cover pie. Using a 1cm cutter, cut out rounds from pastry, reserving rounds. Place pastry over filling, trim edge with a knife. Place rounds on pastry, brush a little of the lightly beaten egg white over pastry; sprinkle with sugar. Place pie on an oven tray.

6 Bake pie about 30 minutes or until well browned. (Cover the edges of the pastry with foil after 20 minutes to prevent over-browning). Stand 10 minutes before serving with double cream, if you like.

prep + cook time 3 hours
(+ refrigeration)
serves 8
nutritional count per serving
11.6g fat; 493 cal (2061kJ)

BERRY & RHUBARB PIES

220g coarsely chopped rhubarb
55g caster sugar
2 tablespoons water
1 tablespoon cornflour
300g frozen mixed berries
1 egg white
2 teaspoons caster sugar, extra
pastry
250g plain flour
75g caster sugar
150g cold butter, chopped
   coarsely
1 egg yolk

1 Make pastry.
2 Place rhubarb, sugar and half the water in medium saucepan; bring to the boil. Reduce heat; simmer, covered, about 3 minutes or until rhubarb is tender. Blend cornflour with the remaining water; stir into rhubarb mixture. Stir over heat until mixture boils and thickens. Remove from heat; stir in berries. Cool.
3 Grease six-hole (180ml) large muffin pan. Roll two-thirds of the pastry between sheets of baking parchment to 4mm thickness; cut out six 12cm rounds. Press rounds into pan holes. Refrigerate 30 minutes.
4 Preheat oven to 200°C/180°C fan-assisted.
5 Roll remaining pastry between sheets of baking parchment to 4mm thickness; cut out six 9cm rounds.
6 Spoon fruit mixture into pastry cases.
7 Brush edge of 9cm rounds with egg white; place over filling. Press edges firmly to seal. Brush tops with egg white; sprinkle with extra sugar.

8 Bake pies about 30 minutes. Stand in pan 10 minutes; using palette knife, loosen pies from edge of pan before lifting out. Serve warm with vanilla ice-cream, if you like.
pastry Process flour, sugar and butter until crumbly. Add egg yolk; process until combined. Knead on floured surface until smooth. Cover; refrigerate 30 minutes.

prep + cook time 1 hour
(+ refrigeration)
makes 6
nutritional count per pie 22.1g fat; 464 cal (1946kJ)
tip If pastry mixture is too dry, add 2 teaspoons of water with the egg yolk.

COUNTRY APPLE PIE

10 medium apples (1.5kg)
125ml water
55g caster sugar
1 teaspoon finely grated lemon
  rind
¼ teaspoon ground cinnamon
1 egg white
1 tablespoon caster sugar, extra
pastry
150g plain flour
75g self-raising flour
35g cornflour
30g custard powder
1 tablespoon caster sugar
100g cold butter, chopped
  coarsely
1 egg yolk
60ml iced water

1 Make pastry.
2 Peel, core and slice apple thickly. Place apple and the water in large saucepan; bring to the boil. Reduce heat; simmer, covered, 10 minutes or until apples soften. Drain; stir in sugar, rind and cinnamon. Cool.
3 Preheat oven to 220°C/200°C fan-assisted. Grease deep 25cm pie dish.
4 Divide pastry in half. Roll one half between sheets of baking parchment until large enough to line dish. Lift pastry into dish; press into base and side. Spoon apple mixture into pastry case; brush edge with egg white.
5 Roll remaining pastry large enough to cover filling; lift onto filling. Press edges together; trim away excess pastry. Brush pastry with egg white; sprinkle with extra sugar.
6 Bake pie 20 minutes. Reduce oven to 180°C/160°C fan-assisted; bake about 25 minutes or until golden brown. Serve with vanilla custard, or scoops of vanilla ice-cream, if you like.

pastry Process dry ingredients with the butter until crumbly. Add egg yolk and the water; process until combined. Knead on floured surface until smooth. Cover; refrigerate 30 minutes.

prep + cook time 1 hour 45 minutes (+ refrigeration)
serves 8
nutritional count per serving 11.4g fat; 344 cal (1438kJ)

APPLE CRANBERRY TURNOVERS

40g butter
4 medium apples (600g), peeled, chopped finely
55g brown sugar
45g dried cranberries
35g coarsely chopped roasted walnuts
1 teaspoon ground cinnamon
2 teaspoons lemon juice
12 sheets filo pastry
75g butter, melted

1 Melt butter in large frying pan; cook apple, stirring, about 10 minutes or until apple is tender. Add sugar; stir until dissolved. Remove from heat, stir in cranberries, nuts, cinnamon and juice. Cool.
2 Preheat oven to 220°C/200°C fan-assisted. Grease oven trays.
3 Place four sheets of pastry on top of each other; cover remaining sheets with baking parchment then a damp tea towel. Cut six 12cm rounds from pastry. Brush between each layer of pastry with some of the melted butter. Repeat with remaining sheets (you will have 18 pastry rounds).
4 Divide apple mixture among pastry rounds. Fold over pastry to enclose filling, pressing edges together. Brush turnovers with remaining butter.
5 Bake turnovers about 8 minutes or until browned lightly. Serve turnovers immediately with ice-cream, if you like.

prep + cook time 45 minutes
makes 18
nutritional count per turnover
6.8g fat; 119 cal (497kJ)

SPICED STONE FRUIT STRUDEL

2 medium peaches (300g),
  quartered, sliced thinly
2 medium nectarines (340g),
  quartered, sliced thinly
2 tablespoons brown sugar
80g sultanas
1½ teaspoons ground cinnamon
½ teaspoon ground nutmeg
25g fresh breadcrumbs
6 sheets filo pastry
20g butter, melted
2 tablespoons milk
2 teaspoons icing sugar

1 Combine peach, nectarine, brown sugar, sultanas, spices and breadcrumbs in medium bowl.
2 Preheat oven to 200°C/180°C fan-assisted. Grease oven tray; line with baking parchment.
3 Stack filo sheets, brushing all sheets with half of the combined butter and milk. Cut filo stack in half widthways; cover one stack with baking parchment, then with a damp tea towel, to prevent drying out.
4 Place half of the fruit mixture along centre of uncovered filo stack; roll from one side to enclose filling, sealing ends of roll with a little of the remaining butter mixture. Place strudel, seam-side down, on tray; brush all over with a little of the remaining butter mixture. Repeat process with remaining filo stack, fruit mixture and butter mixture.
5 Bake strudels about 25 minutes or until browned. Cut each strudel in half widthways; divide among plates, dust with sifted icing sugar.

prep + cook time 45 minutes
serves 4
nutritional count per serving 5.5g fat; 285 cal (1191kJ)

PISTACHIO ORANGE PIE

185g coarsely chopped unsalted
  pistachios
1 tablespoon plain flour
2 tablespoons brown sugar
40g butter, melted
2 eggs
180ml maple syrup
2 teaspoons finely grated orange
  rind
1 tablespoon orange juice
2 tablespoons orange marmalade,
  warmed, sieved
pastry
185g plain flour
55g icing sugar
125g cold butter, chopped
  coarsely
1 egg yolk
1 teaspoon iced water,
  approximately

1 Make pastry.
2 Grease 24cm loose-based flan tin. Roll pastry between sheets of baking parchment until large enough to line tin. Ease pastry into tin, press into base and side; trim edge. Cover; refrigerate 30 minutes.
3 Preheat oven to 180°C/160°C fan-assisted.
4 Place tin on oven tray. Line pastry case with baking parchment; fill with dried beans or rice. Bake 10 minutes; remove paper and beans. Bake further 5 minutes; cool.
5 Reduce oven to 160°C/140°C fan-assisted.
6 Combine nuts, flour, sugar, butter, eggs, syrup, rind and juice in medium bowl. Pour mixture into pastry case.
7 Bake pie about 45 minutes. Cool. Brush pie with marmalade.
pastry Process flour, icing sugar and butter until crumbly. Add egg yolk and enough of the water to process until ingredients come together. Knead dough on floured surface until smooth. Cover; refrigerate 30 minutes.

prep + cook time 1 hour 20 minutes (+ refrigeration)
serves 10
nutritional count per serving
23.7g fat; 427 cal (1785kJ)

LEMON CHIFFON PIE

180g digestive biscuit crumbs
125g butter, melted
filling
4 eggs, separated
75g caster sugar
3 teaspoons gelatine
2 teaspoons grated lemon rind
80ml lemon juice
80ml water
75g caster sugar, extra

1 Combine biscuit crumbs and butter in medium bowl. Press mixture firmly over base and side of 23cm pie plate; refrigerate 30 minutes or until firm.
2 Meanwhile, make filling.
3 Spread filling into crumb crust; refrigerate several hours or until set.
filling Stir egg yolks, caster sugar, gelatine, rind, juice and the water in medium heatproof bowl over medium saucepan of simmering water until mixture has thickened slightly. Remove from heat; pour into large bowl. Cover; cool to room temperature. Mixture should be set to about the consistency of unbeaten egg white before remaining ingredients are added. Beat egg whites in small bowl with electric mixer until soft peaks form; add extra sugar gradually, beating until dissolved after additions. Fold egg white mixture through lemon mixture in two batches.

prep + cook time 40 minutes (+ refrigeration & standing)
serves 8
nutritional count per serving 19.4g fat; 337 cal (1409kJ)

LIME MERINGUE PIE

250g digestive biscuits
100g unsalted butter, melted
75g cornflour
330g caster sugar
125ml lime juice
310ml water
60g unsalted butter, extra
4 eggs, separated
2 teaspoons finely grated lime
  rind

1 Grease 24cm loose-based flan tin.

2 Blend or process biscuits until mixture resembles fine breadcrumbs. Add butter; process until combined. Press biscuit mixture evenly over base and 2cm up the side of tin; place on oven tray. Refrigerate until required.

3 Combine cornflour and 110g of the sugar in medium saucepan; gradually stir in juice and the water until smooth. Cook, stirring, over high heat until mixture boils and thickens. Reduce heat; simmer, stirring, 1 minute. Remove from heat; stir in extra butter, then yolks and rind. Continue stirring until butter melts. Cool 10 minutes.

4 Spread filling over biscuit base. Cover; refrigerate 2 hours.

5 Preheat oven to 200°C/180°C fan-assisted.

6 Beat egg whites in small bowl with electric mixer until soft peaks form; gradually add remaining sugar, 1 tablespoon at a time, beating until sugar dissolves between additions.

7 Roughen surface of filling with a fork before spreading with meringue mixture. Bake about 5 minutes or until meringue is browned lightly.

prep + cook time 30 minutes (+ refrigeration)
serves 10
nutritional count per serving 19.8g fat; 420 cal (1756kJ)

BLACK BOTTOM PIE

90g butter
55g caster sugar
1 egg
150g plain flour
35g self-raising flour
125ml whipping cream
30g dark eating chocolate,
  grated
filling
1 tablespoon gelatine
60ml milk
55g caster sugar
3 teaspoons cornflour
250ml milk, extra
3 eggs, separated
60g dark eating chocolate,
  melted
1 teaspoon vanilla extract
55g caster sugar, extra

1 Beat butter and sugar in small bowl with electric mixer until just combined. Beat in egg. Stir in sifted flours, in two batches. Turn dough onto floured surface; knead until smooth. Cover; refrigerate 30 minutes.
2 Meanwhile, make filling.
3 Preheat oven to 200°C/180°C fan-assisted. Roll pastry on floured surface until large enough to line 23cm pie plate. Ease pastry into plate, press into base and side; trim edge. Prick pastry all over with fork.
4 Bake pastry case 15 minutes or until browned; cool.
5 Spread chocolate custard into pastry case; refrigerate until firm. Spread vanilla custard into pastry case; refrigerate until firm. Spread whipped cream over custard, then sprinkle with grated chocolate.

filling Sprinkle gelatine over milk in small jug. Blend sugar and cornflour with extra milk in small saucepan; stir over heat until mixture boils and thickens, remove from heat. Quickly stir in egg yolks, then gelatine mixture; stir until smooth. Divide custard into two bowls. Stir chocolate into one bowl. Cover both bowls; cool to room temperature. Stir extract into plain custard. Beat egg whites in small bowl with electric mixer until soft peaks form; gradually add extra sugar, beating until dissolved after additions. Fold egg white mixture into vanilla custard, in two batches.

prep + cook time 1 hour
(+ refrigeration)
serves 8
nutritional count per serving
23g fat; 432 cal (1806kJ)

SAVOURY TARTS

LEEK QUICHE

45g butter
4 sheets filo pastry
4 small leeks (800g)
45g butter, extra
1 clove garlic, crushed
125g feta cheese
160ml single cream
3 eggs, beaten lightly

1 Preheat oven to 180°C/160°C fan-assisted.
2 Melt butter; brush each layer of pastry with melted butter, fold each layer over in half. Layer pastry, one folded piece on top of the other to give eight layers. Place pie plate (base measurement 18cm) upside down on layered pastry; using plate as a guide, cut around plate making circle 1cm larger than the plate. Carefully lift all layers of pastry into plate, leave pastry standing up around edge of plate.
3 Trim ends of leeks, leave about 5cm of the green tops; slice leeks finely, wash well under cold running water, drain well.
4 Melt extra butter in pan; cook leek and garlic, stirring, about 5 minutes over low heat until leeks are just tender. Stir in sieved cheese, cream and eggs; season with ground black pepper. Pour mixture into pastry case.
5 Bake quiche about 45 minutes or until golden brown.

prep + cook time 1 hour 15 minutes
serves 6
nutritional count per serving 32.2g fat; 376 cal (1572kJ)

TOMATO & BASIL QUICHE

150g plain flour
75g butter, chopped
1 egg yolk
1 tablespoon lemon juice,
    approximately
30g butter, extra
1 medium leek (350g), sliced
    thinly
3 eggs
300ml single cream
90g grated cheddar cheese
3 small ripe tomatoes (270g),
    peeled, cut into 1cm slices
6 tablespoons coarsely chopped
    fresh basil
2 handfuls coarsely chopped flat-
    leaf parsley
1 tablespoon finely grated
    parmesan cheese

1 Sift flour into bowl, rub in chopped butter. Add egg yolk and enough juice to mix to firm dough. Cover; refrigerate 30 minutes.
2 Preheat oven to 200°C/180°C fan-assisted. Grease 23cm flan tin.
3 Roll pastry on floured surface until large enough to line flan tin. Ease pastry into tin, press into base and side; trim edge. Line tin with baking parchment; fill with dried beans or rice. Bake about 10 minutes. Remove paper and beans; bake further 5 minutes.
4 Meanwhile, melt extra butter in medium frying pan; cook leek, stirring, until tender. Combine eggs, cream and cheese in medium bowl, stir in leek mixture; pour into pastry case. Roll edge of tomato slices in combined basil and parsley, place on top of leek mixture; sprinkle with cheese. Bake quiche about 30 minutes.

prep + cook time 45 minutes
(+ refrigeration)
serves 8
nutritional count per serving
47.7g fat; 572 cal (2391kJ)

SUN-DRIED TOMATO & COURGETTE QUICHE

100g cottage cheese
100g butter, softened
200g plain flour
1 tablespoon olive oil
1 medium brown onion (150g),
  sliced thinly
35g drained, finely chopped
  sun-dried tomatoes
70g drained sun-dried courgettes
3 tablespoons finely shredded
  fresh basil leaves
60g grated gruyère cheese
20g grated parmesan cheese
3 eggs
180ml single cream
30g grated cheddar cheese

1 Combine cottage cheese and butter in large bowl; stir in flour. Press dough into ball; knead gently on floured surface until smooth. Cover; refrigerate 30 minutes.

2 Preheat oven to 200°C/180°C fan-assisted.

3 Roll dough on floured surface until large enough to line 24cm flan tin. Ease pastry into tin; trim edge. Place tin on oven tray. Line pastry with baking parchment; fill with dried beans or rice. Bake 10 minutes. Remove paper and beans; bake further 10 minutes or until browned.

4 Reduce oven to 180°C/160°C fan-assisted.

5 Heat oil in medium saucepan; cook onion, stirring, until soft. Drain on absorbent paper.

6 Spread onion, tomato, courgettes, basil, gruyère and parmesan into pastry case. Top with combined eggs and cream; sprinkle with cheddar cheese. Bake quiche about 35 minutes or until set.

prep + cook time 1 hour
(+ refrigeration)
serves 6
nutritional count per serving
40.6g fat; 550 cal (2299kJ)

QUICHE LORRAINE

1 medium brown onion (150g), chopped finely
3 rashers rindless bacon (195g), chopped finely
3 eggs
300ml single cream
125ml milk
120g coarsely grated gruyère cheese
pastry
260g plain flour
150g cold butter, chopped coarsely
1 egg yolk
2 teaspoons lemon juice
80ml iced water, approximately

1 Make pastry.
2 Preheat oven to 200°C/180°C fan-assisted.
3 Roll pastry between sheets of baking parchment until large enough to line a deep 23cm loose-based flan tin. Lift pastry into tin; gently press pastry around side. Trim edge, place tin on oven tray. Cover pastry with baking parchment; fill with dried beans or rice. Bake 10 minutes; remove paper and beans. Bake pastry a further 10 minutes or until golden brown; cool.
4 Reduce oven temperature to 180°C/160°C fan-assisted.
5 Cook onion and bacon in heated oiled small frying pan until onion is soft; drain on absorbent paper, cool. Sprinkle bacon mixture over pastry case.
6 Whisk eggs in medium bowl then whisk in cream, milk and cheese; pour into pastry case. Bake about 35 minutes or until filling is set. Stand 5 minutes before removing quiche from tin.

pastry Sift flour into bowl; rub in butter. Add egg yolk, juice and enough water to make ingredients cling together. Knead gently on floured surface until smooth. Cover; refrigerate 30 minutes.

prep + cook time 1 hour 30 minutes (+ refrigeration)
serves 6
nutritional count per serving 51.8g fat; 751 cal (3139kJ)

MOROCCAN TART

1 sheet shortcrust pastry
1 tablespoon olive oil
300g minced lamb
1 teaspoon ground coriander
½ teaspoon ground cinnamon
400g can chickpeas, rinsed,
   drained
1 clove garlic, crushed
2 tablespoons lemon juice
1 piece preserved lemon (35g),
   trimmed, chopped finely
2 tablespoons roasted pine nuts
125g feta cheese, crumbled

1 Preheat oven to 200°C/180°C fan-assisted. Oil oven tray.
2 Roll pastry out to 28cm x 30cm rectangle; place on tray. Fold edges of pastry over to make a 1cm border all the way around pastry. Prick pastry base with fork; bake 10 minutes.
3 Meanwhile, heat half of the oil in medium frying pan; cook lamb, coriander and cinnamon, stirring, 5 minutes. Drain away excess oil.
4 Combine chickpeas, garlic, juice and remaining oil in medium bowl. Using fork, coarsely mash mixture; stir in preserved lemon. Spread over pastry base. Top with lamb mixture; sprinkle with nuts and cheese.
5 Bake tart about 10 minutes.

prep + cook time 45 minutes
serves 4
nutritional count per serving
34.8g fat; 544 cal (2274kJ)

TOMATO, PESTO & OLIVE TART

500g baby plum or cherry
  tomatoes
1 tablespoon balsamic vinegar
1 tablespoon olive oil
1 sheet puff pasty
2 tablespoons basil pesto
55g pitted black olives
360g ricotta cheese

1 Preheat oven to 220°C/200°C fan-assisted.

2 Combine tomatoes in medium bowl with vinegar and half the oil; spread tomatoes on oven tray. Roast, uncovered, about 10 minutes or until tomatoes collapse.

3 Place pastry on oiled oven tray. Fold edges of pastry over to make a 5mm border all the way around pastry; prick base with fork. Place another oven tray on top of pastry; bake 10 minutes. Remove top tray from pastry. Reduce oven to 200°C/180°C fan-assisted.

4 Spread pastry with pesto; top with tomatoes and olives. Sprinkle with cheese. Bake about 10 minutes. Drizzle with remaining oil before serving.

prep + cook time 30 minutes
serves 4
nutritional count per serving
28.4g fat; 400 cal (1672kJ)

CLASSIC FRENCH ONION TART

225g plain flour
125g cold butter, chopped
    coarsely
1 egg yolk
2 tablespoons iced water,
    approximately
onion filling
60g butter
1 tablespoon olive oil
5 medium brown onions (750g),
    sliced thinly
pinch ground nutmeg
3 egg yolks
125ml double cream

1 Process flour and butter until mixture is crumbly. Add egg yolk and enough of the water to process until ingredients just come together. Cover; refrigerate 30 minutes.
2 Preheat oven to 200°C/180°C fan-assisted. Grease 22cm fluted loose-based flan tin.
3 Roll dough between sheets of baking parchment until large enough to line tin. Lift pastry into tin, press into base and side, trim edge; prick base all over with fork. Place tin on oven tray; line pastry with baking parchment, fill with dried beans or rice. Bake 10 minutes. Remove paper and beans; bake further 10 minutes. Cool.
4 Meanwhile, make onion filling.
5 Reduce oven temperature to 180°C/160°C fan-assisted.
6 Spread onion mixture into tart shell. Bake about 25 minutes or until set.

onion filling Heat butter and oil in large frying pan; cook onion, covered, stirring occasionally, about 30 minutes or until onion is soft. Remove from heat. Add combined nutmeg, egg yolks and cream; mix well. Season with salt and cracked black pepper.

prep + cook time 1 hour 40 minutes (+ refrigeration & cooling)
serves 8
nutritional count per serving 31.4g fat; 413 cal (1726kJ)

SPINACH & BEETROOT TART

1 sheet puff pasty
250g frozen spinach, thawed, drained
200g feta cheese, crumbled
425g cooked baby beetroot, sliced thinly

1 Preheat oven to 220°C/200°C fan-assisted.
2 Place pastry on an oiled oven tray. Fold edges of pastry over to make a 5mm border all the way around pastry. Prick pastry base with fork. Place another oven tray on top of pastry; bake 10 minutes. Remove top tray from pastry. Reduce oven to 200°C/180°C fan-assisted.
3 Meanwhile, combine spinach with half the cheese in medium bowl.
4 Top pastry with spinach mixture, beetroot and remaining cheese.
5 Bake tart about 10 minutes.

prep + cook time 40 minutes
serves 4
nutritional count per serving
21.4g fat; 340 cal (1421kJ)

SHALLOT TARTS

225g plain flour
125g butter
2 egg yolks
1 tablespoon water,
   approximately
1 egg white, beaten lightly
filling
60g butter
250g shallots, chopped finely
3 eggs, beaten lightly
300ml single cream
30g blue cheese, crumbled

1 Sift flour into bowl, rub in butter. Add egg yolks and enough water to make ingredients cling together. Press dough into a ball, cover; refrigerate 30 minutes.
2 Preheat oven to 200°C/180°C fan-assisted.
3 Roll pastry until large enough to line six 11cm flan tins. Place tins on oven tray. Prick pastry all over with fork; bake about 15 minutes or until golden brown. Brush sides and bases with egg white; cool.
4 Reduce oven to 180°C/160°C fan-assisted.
5 Meanwhile, make filling; pour into cases.
6 Bake tartlets about 15 minutes or until filling is set.
filling Heat butter in frying pan; cook shallots, stirring constantly, until soft; drain on absorbent paper. Cool. Combine egg, cream, crumbled cheese and shallot mixture in medium bowl.

prep + cook time 1 hour
makes 6
nutritional count per tart 53.6g fat; 647 cal (2704kJ)

SWEET TARTS

CRÈME BRÛLÉE TART

225g plain flour
2 tablespoons custard powder
125g cold butter, chopped
1 egg yolk
1 tablespoon cold water,
    approximately
filling
5 egg yolks
75g caster sugar
1 vanilla pod
375ml whipping cream
80ml milk
topping
1½ tablespoons brown sugar
1 tablespoon icing sugar

1 Grease 24cm loose-based flan tin. Process flour, custard powder and butter until just crumbly. Add egg yolk and enough water to make ingredients just cling together. Press dough into a ball, knead on floured surface until smooth. Wrap in cling film; refrigerate 30 minutes.

2 Roll pastry between sheets of baking parchment until large enough to line tin. Lift pastry into tin, ease into base and side; trim edge. Refrigerate 30 minutes.

3 Preheat oven to 200°C/180°C fan-assisted.

4 Line pastry with baking parchment, fill with dried beans or rice; place on oven tray. Bake 10 minutes. Remove paper and beans; bake further 10 minutes or until pastry is lightly browned. Cool.

5 Reduce oven to 150°C/130°C fan-assisted.

6 Meanwhile, make filling. Pour filling into pastry case. Bake tart about 1 hour or until custard is set; cool.

7 Make topping. Sift topping evenly over filling; refrigerate 1 hour.

8 Preheat grill. Cover pastry edge of tart with foil; place under hot grill 2 minutes or until sugar is melted and golden brown. (If sugar does not melt in 2 minutes, lightly brush topping with water and grill again.)

filling Whisk egg yolks and sugar in medium bowl until thick and creamy. Split vanilla pod lengthways, scrape seeds into medium saucepan. Bring cream and milk to the boil in small saucepan; remove from heat. Whisk hot milk mixture into egg yolk mixture; strain. Cool.

topping Sift sugars together twice through a fine sieve.

prep + cook time 1 hour 40 minutes (+ refrigeration & standing)
serves 8
nutritional count per serving 34.6g fat; 484 cal (2023kJ)

TREACLE TART

185g plain flour
40g custard powder
2 tablespoons icing sugar
125g butter, chopped
2 tablespoons milk,
    approximately
filling
100g stale breadcrumbs
360g treacle
2 teaspoons grated lemon rind

1 Sift flour, custard powder and icing sugar into medium bowl, rub in butter. Add enough milk to make ingredients cling together. Press dough into a ball; knead gently on floured surface until smooth. Cover; refrigerate 30 minutes.

2 Preheat oven to 200°C/180°C fan-assisted.

3 Roll two-thirds of the dough between sheets of baking parchment until large enough to line 22cm flan tin. Lift pastry into tin, ease into base and side; trim edge. Place tin on oven tray, line pastry with paper, fill with dried beans or rice. Bake 10 minutes. Remove paper and beans; bake further 10 minutes or until lightly browned. Cool.

4 Reduce oven to 180°C/160°C fan-assisted.

5 Make filling; spread into pastry case.

6 Roll remaining pastry into a rectangle on floured surface; cut into 1cm strips. Brush edge of pastry case with a little extra milk. Place pastry strips over filling in lattice pattern; brush pastry with a little more milk.

7 Bake tart 25 minutes or until pastry is lightly browned. Cool tart in tin. Just before serving, dust with icing sugar, if you like. Serve with whipped cream or ice-cream.

filling Combine all ingredients in medium bowl.

prep + cook time 1 hour
(+ refrigeration & standing)
serves 8
nutritional count per serving
13.8g fat; 387 cal (1618kJ)

CHOCOLATE-BROWNIE CARAMEL TART

150g plain flour
100g cold unsalted butter, chopped
55g caster sugar
75g finely chopped macadamias
1 egg yolk
1 tablespoon icing sugar
caramel filling
60g unsalted butter
400g can sweetened condensed milk
1 tablespoon golden syrup
2 tablespoons single cream
chocolate-brownie topping
80g unsalted butter
110g caster sugar
70g dark eating chocolate, chopped
1 egg, beaten lightly
35g plain flour
1 tablespoon cocoa powder

1 Grease 24cm loose-based flan tin. Process flour and butter until crumbly, add sugar, nuts and egg yolk, process until ingredients just cling together. Knead dough on floured surface until smooth. Press dough over base and side of tin; prick base with fork. Cover; refrigerate 30 minutes.
2 Preheat oven to 200°C/180°C fan-assisted.
3 Line pastry with baking parchment large enough to extend 10cm over edge, tuck paper under tin to completely cover pastry; fill with dried beans or rice. Place tin on oven tray, bake 15 minutes. Remove beans and paper, loosely cover top edge of pastry with greased foil; bake further 8 minutes or until pastry is lightly browned. Cool.
4 Meanwhile, make caramel filling. Spread warm filling into cool pastry case; stand 30 minutes or until cold and firm.
5 Reduce oven to 180°C/160°C fan-assisted.

6 Make chocolate-brownie topping. Pour topping over caramel; bake about 1 hour. Cool tart in tin. Cover; refrigerate 4 hours. Serve with cream and lightly dusted with icing sugar, if liked.
caramel filling Stir ingredients in small saucepan over medium heat about 10 minutes, until caramel becomes golden brown. Cool slightly.
chocolate-brownie topping Melt butter in small saucepan, add sugar; stir over heat, without boiling, until sugar dissolves. Remove from heat; stir in chocolate until melted, then stir in egg, sifted flour and cocoa. Cool.

prep + cook time 1 hour 40 minutes (+ refrigeration)
serves 10
nutritional count per serving 34.5g fat; 571 cal (2387kJ)

CHOCOLATE PISTACHIO TART

70g roasted, unsalted pistachios
100g unsalted butter, softened
110g caster sugar
2 eggs
100g self-raising flour
35g cocoa powder
160g raspberry jam
12 roasted, unsalted pistachios,
  extra
40g dark eating chocolate,
  melted
pastry
185g plain flour
80g icing sugar
125g cold unsalted butter,
  chopped coarsely
2 tablespoons iced water,
  approximately

1 Make pastry; cover, refrigerate 30 minutes.
2 Grease 12.5cm x 35cm (or 22cm round) loose-based fluted flan tin. Reserve one-quarter of the dough for decoration. Roll remaining dough between sheets of baking parchment until large enough to line tin. Ease dough into tin; press into base and sides. Trim edges; prick base all over with a fork. Refrigerate 30 minutes.
3 Roll out reserved dough on a floured surface, cut out 12 x 2cm rounds; place on a tray lined with baking parchment. Refrigerate 30 minutes.
4 Preheat oven to 200°C/180°C fan-assisted.
5 Blend or process nuts finely.
6 Beat butter and sugar in small bowl with electric mixer until light and fluffy. Beat in eggs, one at a time. Transfer mixture to medium bowl; stir in sifted flour and cocoa, and nuts. Spread jam over base of pastry case; top with pistachio filling. Place pastry rounds on filling. Bake 15 minutes.
7 Reduce oven to 180°C/160°C fan-assisted; bake further 25 minutes. Cool in tin.

8 Dip extra nuts in chocolate; place on pastry rounds. Cool before slicing.
pastry Process sifted flour and sugar with butter until crumbly. Add enough of the water until ingredients just come together when processed. Knead dough on floured surface until smooth.

prep + cook time 1 hour 15 minutes (+ refrigeration)
serves 12
nutritional count per serving
21.4g fat; 396 cal (1655kJ)

BAKED PASSIONFRUIT TART

225g plain flour
55g icing sugar
150g cold unsalted butter,
  chopped
2 egg yolks
filling
7 egg yolks
220g caster sugar
1 teaspoon finely grated lemon
  rind
80ml passionfruit pulp
250ml whipping cream

1 Process flour, sugar and butter until crumbly. Add egg yolks, process until ingredients just come together. Knead dough on floured surface until smooth. Wrap in cling film; refrigerate 30 minutes.
2 Roll pastry between sheets of baking parchment until large enough to line 24cm loose-based flan tin. Ease pastry into base and side of tin; trim edge. Cover; refrigerate 1 hour.
3 Preheat oven to 200°C/180°C fan-assisted.
4 Line pastry with baking parchment, fill with dried beans or rice. Place tin on oven tray; bake 10 minutes. Remove paper and beans; bake further 10 minutes or until pastry is lightly browned. Cool.
5 Reduce oven to 150°C/130°C fan-assisted.
6 Make filling; pour into pastry case. Bake tart about 1 hour or until just set; cool. Serve at room temperature, dusted with a little sifted icing sugar, if you like.
filling Combine all ingredients in medium bowl.

prep + cook time 1 hour 30 minutes (+ refrigeration & standing)
serves 8
nutritional count per serving 33g fat; 546 cal (2282kJ)
tip You need about 4 passionfruit for this recipe.

BERRY FRANGIPANE TART

1 sheet puff pastry
300g frozen mixed berries
frangipane
80g butter, softened
½ teaspoon vanilla extract
75g caster sugar
2 egg yolks
1 tablespoon plain flour
120g ground almonds

1 Preheat oven to 220°C/200°C fan-assisted. Grease 20cm x 30cm baking tin.
2 Roll pastry until large enough to cover base and sides of tin. Line tin with pastry, press into sides. Prick pastry all over with fork; freeze 5 minutes.
3 Place another baking tin on top of pastry; bake 5 minutes. Remove top tin; bake about 5 minutes or until pastry is browned lightly. Cool 5 minutes. Reduce oven to 180°C/160°C fan-assisted.
4 Meanwhile, make frangipane.
5 Spread frangipane over pastry base. Sprinkle with berries, press into frangipane. Bake about 30 minutes or until browned lightly.
frangipane Beat butter, extract, sugar and egg yolks in small bowl with electric mixer until light and fluffy. Stir in flour and ground almonds.

prep + cook time 45 minutes
serves 6
nutritional count per serving 30.2g fat; 412 cal (1722kJ)

LINZER TORTE

150g plain flour
75g self-raising flour
½ teaspoon ground cinnamon
¼ teaspoon ground nutmeg
60g ground almonds
2 tablespoons sugar
125g butter, chopped
1 egg yolk
2 tablespoons water,
   approximately
320g raspberry jam

1 Preheat oven to 180°C/160°C fan-assisted.
2 Sift flours and spices into medium bowl, add almonds and sugar; rub in butter until mixture resembles fine breadcrumbs. Add egg yolk and enough of the water to mix to a firm dough. Knead dough on floured surface until smooth.
3 Roll two-thirds of the pastry thinly between sheets of baking parchment, large enough to fit 23cm flan tin. Lift pastry into tin, ease into base and side; trim edge. Spread base with jam.
4 Roll remaining pastry between sheets of baking parchment, cut into 1cm strips. Arrange pastry strips in a lattice pattern over jam.
5 Bake torte about 45 minutes or until pastry is lightly browned. Serve torte warm or cold.

prep + cook time 1 hour 15 minutes
serves 8
nutritional count per serving 17.9g fat; 384 cal (1605kJ)

ALMOND JALOUSIE

375g packet puff pastry
1 tablespoon apricot jam
1 egg white
2 teaspoons caster sugar
almond filling
30g butter
80g flaked almonds
2 tablespoons caster sugar
1 teaspoon vanilla extract
2 egg yolks
2 teaspoons plain flour

1 Make almond filling.
2 Preheat oven to 220°C/200°C fan-assisted.
3 Cut pastry in half, roll one half into neatly trimmed 12cm x 25cm rectangle; place on oven tray. Spread warmed sieved jam over centre. Place almond filling on pastry leaving a 2cm border around the edge.
4 Roll remaining pastry into a neatly trimmed 13cm x 27cm rectangle; fold in half lengthways. Brush pastry on both sides with egg white. Cut through folded edge of pastry at 2cm intervals leaving a 2cm border down long side of pastry strip.
5 Brush around edge of pastry strip on oven tray with egg white. Carefully unfold cut pastry strip, place over almond filling. Press edges of pastry together using thumb and back of knife to make decorative edge. Brush evenly with egg white, sprinkle with sugar. Bake 5 minutes.
6 Reduce oven to 200°C/180°C fan-assisted; bake for further 10 minutes or until golden brown.

almond filling Melt butter in small saucepan; cook almonds, stirring constantly, over heat until browned lightly. Process almond mixture with remaining ingredients until smooth.

prep + cook time 35 minutes (+ standing)
serves 8
nutritional count per serving 20.3g fat; 309 cal (1292kJ)
tip Jalousie is best made on the day of serving. Serve with whipped cream, if you like.

APPLE GALETTE

500g packet puff pastry roll
4 large apples (800g), cored
2 tablespoons lemon juice
1 tablespoon caster sugar
60g butter, chopped
2 tablespoons apricot jam,
    warmed, sieved

1 Preheat oven to 240°C/220°C fan-assisted.
2 Cut a 35cm length from puff pastry roll; place on oven tray. Turn edges in about 2cm, press lightly.
3 Thinly slice whole apples, toss in juice; place on pastry. Sprinkle with sugar, dot with half the butter.
4 Place galette in oven; reduce to 200°C/180°C fan-assisted, bake 20 minutes. Dot galette with remaining butter; bake further 25 minutes or until browned. Brush hot galette with jam. Serve warm or cold with whipped cream, if you like.

prep + cook time 1 hour
serves 6
nutritional count per serving 26.9g fat; 465 cal (1944kJ)
tip We used a combination of granny smith and red-skinned apples in this recipe.

NECTARINE & MACADAMIA TART

185g plain flour
2 tablespoons caster sugar
90g cold butter, chopped
1 egg yolk
½ teaspoon vanilla extract
2 teaspoons cold water,
    approximately
3 medium nectarines (500g),
    cut into eighths
macadamia filling
110g macadamias
35g plain flour
75g butter
75g brown sugar
1 egg
1 egg yolk
2 tablespoons maple syrup

1 Blend or process flour, sugar and butter until combined. Add egg yolk, extract and enough of the water to make ingredients just come together. Knead dough on floured surface until smooth. Enclose in cling film; refrigerate 30 minutes.
2 Roll dough between sheets of baking parchment until large enough to line base and side of 24cm loose-based flan tin. Ease dough into tin; trim edge. Place tin on oven tray; cover, refrigerate 30 minutes.
3 Meanwhile, preheat oven to 180°C/160°C fan-assisted.
4 Line pastry case with baking parchment; fill with dried beans or rice. Bake 20 minutes; remove paper and beans. Bake about 5 minutes or until browned lightly.
5 Meanwhile, make macadamia filling.
6 Spread filling into pastry case; arrange nectarine segments over filling.
7 Bake tart about 35 minutes or until golden brown and firm to touch. Cool.

macadamia filling Process macadamias and 2 tablespoons of the flour until fine. Beat butter and sugar in small bowl with electric mixer until pale. Beat in egg and egg yolk until combined; fold in syrup, macadamia mixture and remaining flour.

prep + cook time 1 hour 15 minutes (+ refrigeration)
serves 8
nutritional count per serving 29.7g fat; 464 cal (1940kJ)

MINI MOUTHFULS

LITTLE CHICKEN & LEEK PIES

180ml chicken stock
125ml dry white wine
2 chicken breast fillets (340g)
20g butter
1 medium leek (350g), chopped finely
1 stalk celery (150g), trimmed, chopped finely
1 tablespoon plain flour
2 teaspoons fresh lemon thyme leaves
125ml single cream
1 teaspoon dijon mustard
4 sheets shortcrust pastry
3 sheets puff pastry
1 egg yolk, beaten lightly
lemon thyme leaves, extra

1 Bring stock and wine to the boil in medium saucepan. Add chicken; return to the boil. Cover; reduce heat, simmer about 10 minutes or until chicken is just cooked through. Remove from heat; stand chicken 10 minutes. Remove chicken, reserve 180ml cooking liquid; chop chicken finely.
2 Melt butter in medium saucepan; cook leek and celery, stirring, until soft. Add flour and thyme, stir until bubbling. Gradually stir in reserved cooking liquid and cream; cook, stirring, until mixture boils and thickens. Stir in chicken and mustard. Remove from heat, cool slightly.
3 Preheat oven to 220°C/200°C fan-assisted. Grease three 12-hole patty pans.
4 Using 7cm cutter, cut 36 rounds from shortcrust pastry. Press into pan holes. Spoon 1 tablespoon of chicken mixture into each pastry case.

5 Using 6cm cutter, cut 36 rounds from puff pastry. Top chicken mixture with pastry lids, brush with egg yolk and sprinkle with extra thyme.
6 Bake pies about 15 minutes or until browned.

prep + cook time 1 hour (+ cooling)
makes 36
nutritional count per pie 10.5g fat; 171 cal (715kJ)

CHICKEN & OLIVE EMPANADAS

500ml chicken stock
1 bay leaf
3 chicken thigh fillets (330g)
1 tablespoon olive oil
1 small brown onion (80g),
    chopped finely
2 cloves garlic, crushed
2 teaspoons ground cumin
80g sultanas
40g coarsely chopped pitted
    green olives
5 sheets shortcrust pastry
1 egg, beaten lightly

1 Place stock and bay leaf in medium frying pan; bring to the boil. Add chicken, reduce heat; poach chicken, covered, about 10 minutes or until cooked through. Cool chicken in liquid 10 minutes; shred chicken finely. Reserve 250ml of the poaching liquid; discard remainder.
2 Meanwhile, heat oil in large frying pan; cook onion, stirring, until softened. Add garlic and cumin; cook, stirring, until fragrant. Add sultanas and reserved poaching liquid; bring to the boil. Reduce heat; simmer, uncovered, about 15 minutes or until liquid is almost evaporated. Stir in chicken and olives.
3 Preheat oven to 200°C/180°C fan-assisted. Grease two oven trays.
4 Using 9cm cutter, cut 24 rounds from pastry sheets. Place 1 level tablespoon of the filling in centre of each round; fold round in half to enclose filling, pinching edges to seal. Using fork, press around edges of empanadas. Place on trays; brush tops with egg.
5 Bake empanadas about 25 minutes. Serve with yogurt.

prep + cook time 45 minutes
makes 24
nutritional count per empanada
12g fat; 203 cal (849kJ)

CREAMY SMOKED SALMON TARTLETS

3 sheets puff pastry
100g smoked salmon, chopped
    finely
2 gherkins, chopped finely
2 spring onions, chopped finely
120g soured cream
1 tablespoon milk
2 eggs, beaten lightly
1 teaspoon finely chopped fresh
    dill
¼ teaspoon hot paprika

1 Preheat oven to 180°C/160°C fan-assisted. Grease two 12-hole shallow patty pans.
2 Cut 24 x 6.5cm rounds from pastry; place into patty pan holes.
3 Sprinkle salmon, gherkin and onion into pastry cases; pour in combined soured cream, milk, egg, dill and paprika.
4 Bake tartlets about 30 minutes. Serve hot.

prep + cook time 45 minutes
makes 24
nutritional count per tartlet
7.4g fat; 111 cal (464kJ)

MINI BEEF & GUINNESS PIES

1 tablespoon vegetable oil
500g beef skirt steak, chopped
   finely
1 medium brown onion (150g),
   chopped finely
2 tablespoons plain flour
375ml bottled draught Guinness
250ml beef stock
5 sheets shortcrust pastry
1 egg, beaten lightly

1 Heat oil in large saucepan; cook beef, stirring, until browned. Add onion; cook, stirring, until softened. Add flour; cook, stirring, until mixture bubbles and is well browned.
2 Gradually add Guinness and stock, stirring until gravy boils and thickens. Cover, reduce heat; simmer, stirring occasionally, 1 hour. Uncover; simmer, stirring occasionally, 30 minutes. Cool filling 10 minutes then refrigerate until cold.
3 Preheat oven to 220°C/200°C fan-assisted. Grease three 12-hole mini (20ml) muffin pans.
4 Using 6cm pastry cutter, cut 36 rounds from pastry sheets; place one round in each of the muffin pan holes. Using 5cm pastry cutter, cut 36 rounds from remaining pastry sheets.
5 Spoon a heaped teaspoon of the cold filling into each pastry case; brush around edges with egg. Top each pie with smaller pastry round, press gently around edge to seal; brush with remaining egg. Using sharp knife, make two small slits in top of each pie.
6 Bake pies about 15 minutes or until browned lightly. Stand 5 minutes in pan before placing on serving platters.

prep + cook time 2 hours
(+ refrigeration)
makes 36
nutritional count per pie
7.4g fat; 135 cal (564kJ)

PROSCIUTTO & ROASTED PEPPER QUICHES

6 slices prosciutto (90g)
3 sheets shortcrust pastry
4 slices (170g) bottled roasted
  red pepper, chopped coarsely
4 tablespoons coarsely chopped
  fresh basil
75g grated pizza cheese
quiche filling
300ml single cream
60ml milk
3 eggs

1 Preheat oven to 200°C/180°C fan-assisted. Grease 12-hole (80ml) muffin pan.
2 Cook prosciutto in heated oiled large frying pan until crisp. Cool; chop coarsely.
3 Make quiche filling.
4 Cut twelve 9cm rounds from pastry; press into pan holes. Divide combined prosciutto, pepper, basil and cheese among pastry cases; pour quiche filling into pastry cases.
5 Bake quiches about 25 minutes. Stand in pan 5 minutes before serving.
quiche filling Whisk ingredients in large jug.

prep + cook time 45 minutes
makes 12
nutritional count per quiche
26.5g fat; 350 cal (1462kJ)

GORGONZOLA & FENNEL TARTLETS

120g gorgonzola cheese,
  crumbled
120g soured cream
2 eggs
1 tablespoon olive oil
2 small fennel (600g), trimmed,
  halved, sliced thinly
4 sheets filo pastry
cooking-oil spray

1 Blend or process cheese, soured cream and eggs until smooth; transfer to large jug.
2 Heat oil in small frying pan; cook fennel, stirring, until soft.
3 Preheat oven to 180°C/160°C fan-assisted. Lightly oil two 12-hole mini (20ml) muffin pans.
4 Cut pastry into 7cm squares. Stack two squares of pastry on board; spray with oil. Place another two squares diagonally on top to make star shape; spray with oil. Press into hole of mini muffin pan; repeat with remaining pastry.
5 Divide cheese mixture among pastry cases; top with fennel. Bake, uncovered, about 15 minutes or until filling sets and pastry is browned lightly. Stand tartlets in pans 5 minutes before serving hot.

prep+ cook time 40 minutes
makes 24
nutritional count per tartlet
5g fat; 61 cal (254kJ)

MUSHROOM & BACON BRUNCH TARTS

4 rashers rindless bacon (260g),
  chopped
125g butter
200g chestnut mushrooms,
  halved
2 teaspoons worcestershire sauce
8 sheets filo pastry
12 small eggs (50g each)
2 tablespoons finely chopped
  fresh chives

1 Preheat oven to 200°C/180°C fan-assisted. Grease 12-hole (80ml) muffin pan.

2 Cook bacon in heated frying pan until just cooked; drain.

3 Heat 30g of the butter in same pan; cook mushrooms, stirring, until browned. Stir in sauce.

4 Melt remaining butter. Brush one pastry sheet with butter, top with another sheet. Repeat with two more sheets of pastry. Cut through the four layers of pastry into 10cm squares. Place one square diagonally over another to give eight points. Press pastry into one pan hole. Repeat with remaining pastry sheets and butter.

5 Break eggs into pastry cases, top with mushroom mixture and bacon.

6 Bake tarts 20 minutes or until pastry is browned. Just before serving, sprinkle tarts with chives and freshly ground black pepper.

prep + cook time 45 minutes
makes 12
nutritional count per tart
15.9g fat; 216 cal (903kJ)

TOMATO, LEEK & MARINATED FETA TARTLETS

1 medium leek (350g)
20g butter
1 tablespoon olive oil
2 sheets puff pastry
250g cherry tomatoes,
 sliced thinly
½ teaspoon fresh thyme leaves
1 tablespoon red wine vinegar
marinated feta
1 teaspoon finely grated lemon
 rind
¼ teaspoon cracked black
 pepper
2 cloves garlic, crushed
2 teaspoons fresh thyme leaves
200g feta cheese, cut into
 24 pieces
310ml olive oil

1 Make marinated feta.
2 Preheat oven to 220°C/200°C fan-assisted. Oil oven trays.
3 Cut leek into 6cm pieces; cut pieces in half lengthways, slice halves lengthways into thin strips. Heat butter and oil in large frying pan; cook leek, stirring occasionally, about 20 minutes or until soft.
4 Meanwhile, cut each pastry sheet into twelve 6cm x 8cm rectangles; place on trays. Fold in each side to form a 2mm border; prick pastry pieces with fork. Bake, uncovered, about 10 minutes or until browned lightly. Remove from oven; using fork, immediately press pastry pieces down to flatten. Reduce oven to 200°C/180°C fan-assisted.
5 Meanwhile, place tomato in medium bowl with thyme and vinegar; toss gently to combine.
6 Spread 1 tablespoon of the leek mixture over each pastry piece; crumble one piece of the cheese over each then top with tomato mixture. Bake about 5 minutes or until tomato just softens. Serve immediately.

marinated feta Combine rind, pepper, garlic and thyme in medium sterilised glass jar with a tight-fitting lid; add cheese. Seal jar then shake gently to coat cheese in mixture. Open jar and pour in enough of the oil to completely cover cheese mixture. Reseal; refrigerate overnight.

prep + cook time 1 hour
(+ refrigeration)
makes 24
nutritional count per tartlet
7.2g fat; 99 cal (414kJ)

BLOOD ORANGE MERINGUE PIES

110g caster sugar
2 tablespoons cornflour
160ml blood orange juice
2 tablespoons water
2 teaspoons finely grated
blood orange rind
75g unsalted butter,
chopped coarsely
2 eggs, separated
110g caster sugar, extra
pastry
185g plain flour
55g caster sugar
125g cold butter, chopped
coarsely
1 egg yolk
2 teaspoons water

1 Make pastry.
2 Grease 12-hole (80ml) muffin pan. Roll pastry between sheets of baking parchment to 4mm thickness; cut out 12 x 8cm rounds. Press rounds into pan holes; prick bases all over with fork. Refrigerate 30 minutes.
3 Preheat oven to 200°C/180°C fan-assisted.
4 Bake pastry cases 10 minutes. Cool.
5 Meanwhile, combine sugar and cornflour in small saucepan; gradually stir in juice and the water until smooth. Cook, stirring, until mixture boils and thickens. Reduce heat; simmer, stirring, 1 minute. Remove from heat; stir in rind, butter and egg yolks. Cool 10 minutes.
6 Spoon filling into pastry cases. Refrigerate 1 hour.
7 Increase oven to 240°C/220°C fan-assisted.
8 Beat egg whites in small bowl with electric mixer until soft peaks form; gradually add extra sugar, beating until sugar dissolves.

9 Roughen surface of filling with fork; using star nozzle, pipe meringue over filling. Bake about 3 minutes or until browned lightly.
pastry Process flour, sugar and butter until coarse. Add egg yolk and the water; process until combined. Knead on floured surface until smooth. Enclose in cling film; refrigerate 30 minutes.

prep + cook time 45 minutes (+ refrigeration)
makes 12
nutritional count per pie
15.3g fat; 299 cal (1250kJ)

MINI BERRY PIES

300g frozen mixed berries
55g caster sugar
2 teaspoons cornflour
1 tablespoon water
5 sheets shortcrust pastry
1 egg white
1 tablespoon caster sugar, extra

1 Preheat oven to 200°C/180°C fan-assisted. Grease three 12-hole (20ml) mini muffin pans.
2 Stir berries and sugar in small saucepan over heat until sugar dissolves. Bring to the boil. Blend cornflour with the water; stir into berry mixture. Stir over heat until mixture boils and thickens. Cool.
3 Cut 36 x 6cm rounds from pastry; press rounds into pan holes. Cut 36 x 4cm rounds from remaining pastry. Spoon berry mixture into pastry cases; top with rounds. Press edges firmly to seal. Brush tops with egg white; sprinkle with extra sugar. Make small cut in top of each pie.
4 Bake pies about 20 minutes. Stand in pan 10 minutes before turning, top-side up, onto wire rack. Serve pies warm or cold.

prep + cook time 45 minutes
makes 36
nutritional count per pie
6.4g fat; 117 cal (489kJ)

LEMON DELICIOUS TARTLETS

1 sheet puff pastry
20g butter, melted
1 teaspoon caster sugar
2 tablespoons icing sugar
1 egg, separated
75g caster sugar, extra
10g butter, melted, extra
80ml milk
1 teaspoon finely grated lemon
rind
1½ tablespoons lemon juice
2 tablespoons self-raising flour

1 Cut pastry sheet in half; stand on board 5 minutes or until partially thawed. Grease a 12-hole, deep patty pan tray with a pastry brush dipped in the melted butter. Cut 12 x 10cm squares of baking parchment.

2 Sprinkle one half of pastry with caster sugar, top with remaining pastry half. Roll pastry stack up tightly from short side. Refrigerate until firm.

3 Cut pastry log into 12 x 1cm-wide pieces. Place one pastry piece, spiral-side down, on an icing sugar dusted board; refrigerate remaining pastry pieces. Roll out pastry piece to about 10cm round. Cut out a round from pastry using a 9cm cutter. Press round into a pan hole. Repeat with remaining pastry pieces. Freeze 10 minutes.

4 Preheat oven to 220°C/200°C fan-assisted.

5 Line pastry in pan with baking parchment squares; place about a tablespoon of dried beans or rice. Bake 10 minutes; remove paper and beans. Reduce oven to 160°C/140°C fan-assisted;

bake further 10 minutes or until base of pastry is browned lightly and crisp. Cool. Reduce oven to 150°C/130°C fan-assisted.

6 Meanwhile, beat egg yolk and 2 tablespoons of the extra sugar in a small bowl with an electric mixer until thick and creamy; fold in extra butter, milk, rind and juice, then sifted flour.

7 Beat egg white in small bowl with electric mixer until soft peaks form; gradually beat in remaining extra sugar until sugar dissolves. Fold into lemon mixture, in two batches. Spoon mixture into pastry cases.

8 Bake tartlets 10 minutes or until just set. Remove tartlets from pan; cool on a wire rack. Serve dusted with sifted icing sugar, if you like.

prep + cook time 1 hour
(+ refrigeration)
makes 12
nutritional count per tartlet
6g fat; 121 cal (506kJ)

PORTUGUESE CUSTARD TARTS

110g caster sugar
2 tablespoons cornflour
3 egg yolks
180ml milk
125ml single cream
1 vanilla pod, split lengthways
5cm strip lemon rind
1 sheet butter puff pastry

1 Preheat oven to 220°C/200°C fan-assisted. Grease two 12-hole (20ml) mini muffin pans.
2 Combine sugar and cornflour in medium saucepan. Gradually whisk in combined egg yolks, milk and cream.
3 Scrape vanilla pod seeds into custard; add rind. Stir over medium heat until mixture just comes to the boil. Remove from heat; discard rind. Cover surface of custard with cling film while making pastry cases.
4 Cut pastry sheet in half; place two halves on top of each other. Roll pastry up tightly from long side; cut log into 24 rounds. Roll each round on floured surface to 6cm diameter; press into pan holes.
5 Spoon custard into pastry cases. Bake about 12 minutes. Turn, top-side up, onto wire rack to cool. Serve dusted with a little sifted icing sugar.

prep + cook time 45 minutes (+ standing)
makes 24
nutritional count per tart
4.8g fat; 81 cal (339kJ)

GLOSSARY

almonds

flaked paper-thin slices.

ground also known as almond meal; nuts are powdered to a coarse flour texture.

blood orange a virtually seedless citrus fruit with blood-red-streaked rind and flesh; sweet, non-acidic, salmon-coloured pulp and juice wtih slight strawberry or raspberry overtones. The rind is not as bitter as an ordinary orange.

breadcrumbs, fresh usually white bread, processed into crumbs.

cheese

cottage fresh, white, unripened curd cheese with a lumpy consistency and mild flavour.

feta a crumbly textured goat's- or sheep's-milk cheese with a sharp, salty taste.

gruyère a firm, cow's-milk Swiss cheese having small holes and a nutty, slightly salty flavour. Emmental or appenzeller can be used as a substitute. Available at most supermarkets and delicatessens.

parmesan a sharp-tasting, dry, hard cheese, made from skimmed or semi-skimmed milk and aged for at least a year.

pizza a commercial blend of grated mozzarella, cheddar and parmesan.

ricotta a soft, sweet, moist, white, cow's-milk cheese with a low fat content (about 8.5 per cent) and a slightly grainy texture. The name roughly translates as 'cooked again' and refers to ricotta's manufacture from a whey that is itself a by-product of other cheese making.

chocolate, dark eating made of cocoa liquor, cocoa butter and sugar.

cooking-oil spray we use a cholesterol-free spray made from canola oil.

cornflour also known as cornstarch; used as a thickening agent in cooking.

cream we used fresh cream in this book, unless otherwise stated. Known as single cream or pouring cream, it has no additives unlike commercially thickened cream. Minimum fat content 18%.

double a thick cream containing 48% milk fat.

whipping a cream that contains a thickener. Has a minimum fat content of 35 per cent.

dried cranberries have the same slightly sour, succulent flavour as fresh cranberries. Can usually be substituted for or with other dried fruit in most recipes. Available in most supermarkets. Also available in sweetened form.

fennel bulb vegetable, also known as finocchio or anise. Also the name given to dried seeds having a liquorice flavour.

filo pastry chilled or frozen tissue-thin pastry sheets that are very versatile, lending themselves to both sweet and savoury dishes.

flour

plain all-purpose flour.

self-raising plain flour sifted with baking powder (a raising agent consisting mainly of 2 parts cream of tartar to 1 part bicarbonate of soda) in the proportion of 150g flour to 2 level teaspoons baking powder.

wholemeal also known as wholewheat flour; milled with the wheat germ so is higher in fibre and more nutritional than plain flour.

gelatine we used powdered gelatine; also available in sheet form known as leaf gelatine.

gherkins also known as cornichons; young, dark-green cucumbers grown for pickling.

golden syrup a by-product of refined sugarcane; pure maple syrup or honey can be substituted.

macadamias native to Australia, a rich and buttery nut; store in refrigerator because of its high oil content.

maple syrup distilled from the sap of maple trees found only in Canada and parts of North America. Maple-flavoured syrup is not an adequate substitute for the real thing.

mustard

dijon a pale brown, distinctively flavoured fairly mild French mustard.

english an extremely hot mustard containing ground mustards seeds, flour and tumeric.

wholegrain also known as seeded. A French-style coarse-grain mustard made from crushed mustard seeds and dijon-style French mustard.

olives

black have a richer and more mellow flavour than the green ones and are softer in texture. Sold either plain or in a piquant marinade.

green those harvested before fully ripened and are, as a rule, denser and more bitter than their black relatives.

onions

brown an all-purpose onion, with a light brown skin and yellow flesh.

red a sweet-flavoured, large, purple-red onion.

white has a creamy white flesh and a papery white skin. Their pungent flesh adds flavour to a vast range of dishes.

paprika ground dried red bell pepper (capsicum); available sweet, smoked or hot. Sweet paprika is available at delis, speciality food stores and on line.

passionfruit also known as granadilla; a small tropical fruit, native to Brazil, comprised of a tough dark-purple skin surrounding edible black sweet-sour seeds.

pine nuts also known as pignoli; small, cream-coloured kernels obtained from the cones of different varieties of pine trees.

pistachios pale green, delicately flavoured nut inside hard off-white shells. To peel, soak shelled nuts in boiling water about 5 minutes; drain, then pat dry.

preserved lemon a North African specialty, the lemon is preserved, usually whole, in a mixture of salt and lemon juice or oil. To use, remove and discard pulp, squeeze juice from rind, then rinse rind well before slicing thinly. Available from speciality food shops and delicatessens.

prosciutto salted-cured, air-dried (unsmoked), pressed ham; usually sold in paper-thin slices, ready to eat.

quince a yellow-skinned fruit with hard texture and astringent, tart taste. Once cooked, they turn a deep-pink-ruby-salmon colour.

sauces

soy made from fermented soy beans; several variations are available.

worcestershire a thin, dark-brown, spicy sauce used as seasoning for meat and gravies, and as a condiment.

shallots small, elongated, brown-skinned members of the onion family. Grows in tight clusters similar to garlic.

sugar

caster also known as superfine or finely granulated table sugar.

golden granulated natural brown granulated sugar.

icing also known as confectioners' sugar or powdered sugar.

tomato

paste triple-concentrated tomato purée used to flavour soups, stews, sauces and casseroles.

sun-dried available loose or in packets (not packed in oil).

vanilla

extract obtained from vanilla beans infused in water; a non-alcoholic version of essence.

pod dried long, thin pod from a tropical golden orchid grown in central and South America and Tahiti; the minuscule black seeds inside the bean are used to impart a distinctively sweet vanilla flavour.

INDEX

CONVERSION CHARTS

measures

One metric tablespoon holds 20ml; one metric teaspoon holds 5ml.

All cup and spoon measurements are level. The most accurate way of measuring dry ingredients is to weigh them. When measuring liquids, use a clear glass or plastic jug with metric markings.

We use large eggs with an average weight of 60g.

dry measures

METRIC	IMPERIAL
15g	½oz
30g	1oz
60g	2oz
90g	3oz
125g	4oz (¼lb)
155g	5oz
185g	6oz
220g	7oz
250g	8oz (½lb)
280g	9oz
315g	10oz
345g	11oz
375g	12oz (¾lb)
410g	13oz
440g	14oz
470g	15oz
500g	16oz (1lb)
750g	24oz (1½lb)
1kg	32oz (2lb)

liquid measures

METRIC	IMPERIAL
30ml	1 fluid oz
60ml	2 fluid oz
100ml	3 fluid oz
125ml	4 fluid oz
150ml	5 fluid oz
190ml	6 fluid oz
250ml	8 fluid oz
300ml	10 fluid oz
500ml	16 fluid oz
600ml	20 fluid oz
1000ml (1 litre)	32 fluid oz

length measures

3mm	⅛in
6mm	¼in
1cm	½in
2cm	¾in
2.5cm	1in
5cm	2in
6cm	2½in
8cm	3in
10cm	4in
13cm	5in
15cm	6in
18cm	7in
20cm	8in
23cm	9in
25cm	10in
28cm	11in
30cm	12in (1ft)

oven temperatures

These are fan-assisted temperatures. If you have a conventional oven (ie. not fan-assisted), increase temperatures by 10-20°.

	°C (CELSIUS)	°F (FAHRENHEIT)	GAS MARK
Very low	100	210	½
Low	130	260	1–2
Moderately low	140	280	3
Moderate	160	325	4–5
Moderately hot	180	350	6
Hot	200	400	7–8
Very hot	220	425	9